# TOWARDS YOU, LORD

To Mrs McKibbin
With best wishes
John Frost.
15/10/79.

Books by Flora Larsson

JUST A MOMENT, LORD
MY BEST MEN ARE WOMEN
BETWEEN YOU AND ME, LORD

# TOWARDS YOU, LORD

## PRAYER CONVERSATIONS

by

FLORA LARSSON

HODDER AND STOUGHTON

LONDON SYDNEY AUCKLAND TORONTO

*ISBN 0 340 22815 6.**Printed in Great Britain for Hodder and Stoughton Limited, Mill Road, Dunton Green, Sevenoaks, Kent, by Cox & Wyman Ltd., London, Reading and Fakenham*

# CONTENTS

# GROWING UP

# One dot on a screen

It overwhelms me, Lord!
My head reels at the immensity of life
and my heart fails as I realise that I am
just one faint dot among millions of others
that appear briefly on the screen of history
and pass rapidly without a trace.

*Do I matter?*
That is a vital question for me, Master.
Do *I* matter among so many others?
Does my life count for anything?
I believe it does, Lord, to You,
You, the Creator of life itself, who feel a pang of loss when the fluttering heart of a sparrow ceases to beat.
You have granted me the gift of life,
so I believe I matter to You.

Am I reckoning myself too important?
    Pretending that I am making history
    with my brief sojourn on this planet?
No! oh no, but I believe my life counts with You,
that in some way You will weave my days
    into Your master plan.

Let me be available then,
offering myself and all I have and am
    to Your unknown design.
Even if I am an insignificant thread,
    let me not snap
    so that the fabric is weakened.
Let me play my part, however tiny, however obscure,
    towards the good of the whole.
This, Lord, is my humble prayer.

# Growing pains

Growing pains are real, Lord!
People may regard them as an old wives' tale,
    but they are stark reality;
at any rate in teenage thinking and feeling
    if not in an actual physical sense.

Growing up is painful, Master.
It is a comfort to know that You too
passed through the restless adolescent years,
though that was in a quiet country town
and not in the hurly-burly of modern life
    dominated by TV and radio.

To realise who one is, what one is,
    to be aware of deep new urges
    and awesome possibilities . . .
It's quite frightening, Lord!
The tension between childhood and adulthood
    is pendulum-like in its movement;
one day one thing, the next another.

Be my anchor, Master! Hold me fast
even when I sway between conflicting loyalties
and swing and swoop in changing moods.
Keep me on a steady keel,
    a steady spiritual keel,
until the turbulence of the growing years subsides.
Keep my heart centred on Yourself
    until these temporary storms are over
and I enter adulthood's comparative calm.

# Imprisoned

Master, I'm a prisoner!
I am chained, bound, fettered,
        frustrated by my limitations
        angered by my inabilities . . .
        and I can't escape.

I'm imprisoned in time . . .
The day's relentless hours march on
        forcing me to keep pace
        whipping my lagging feet
flailing me with a fixed programme:
        morning, noon, night . . .
One more day crossed off the calendar.

I'm imprisoned in space . . .
        My own body limits me.
I'm either here or there but never both.
The flesh shackles my liberty,
        encloses and restrains me,
        holds me prisoner,
makes its own demands upon my time and thought.

I'm imprisoned in relationships . . .

Sometimes, though not always, a happy bondage.
The long generations before me look over my shoulder,
casting their amazed or amused glances at me
through the veil of bygone years.
Who I am is inevitably linked with who they were
and what they were.

I'm imprisoned, Master, and often irked by it
yet my spirit is free,
free to wander the world of thought
free to lift to spiritual heights,
daring to reach up to You.
Imprisoned, yet free . . .
Help me to live successfully in that paradox.

## Born good

Lord, it's not fair! Some people are born good,
docile, even-tempered and placid
from early morn to late at night,
from childhood through to old age.
They give me an inferiority complex!
Is their goodness simply a matter of well-functioning
glands?

Why should some of us be storm-centres
with low pressure ever hovering on the horizon?
With cyclones brewing and gale winds threatening
and steam blowing off the lid now and again?
        Is it our own fault
        or can we blame our heritage?

Whatever the cause, what is the remedy, Lord?
At first I seem to hear You say: "Peace!"
All right, I'll quieten down and listen
        to what You have to say.
"You must be born again . . . born of My Spirit" . . .
Is that the secret of a Christian life?
        Not self-mastery, rigidly exercised,
        a daily clenching of the hands,
an agonising remorse when self-control slips,
but rather a new Master in residence,
        a new life within,
        controlled by His Spirit?

Then I see some hope for myself, Lord.
I yield myself to You and Your Spirit.
Take the reins of my life into Your hands
        and guide me through each day.
Change and re-create the inner springs of my being
        by Your presence within my heart,
and as the new comes in, let the old self depart,
        never to reign in power again.

# Inhibited

There is so much locked away inside me, Master,
so much that no-one else knows about but You;
my hopes, desires . . . . and fears.
Why can't I open my heart to someone else
to get advice and counsel?
Why must I bar the door of my being to others,
keeping them out
so that I can hold myself intact within?

Am I afraid of others knowing how I am inside,
learning that I am not always what I seem to be?
Getting to know the real me, perhaps not at all as
acceptable
as the visible image?
What a relief it would be, Lord,
to allow all defences to fall . . .
to talk without reservation
and without fear of misunderstanding
or harsh judgment.

Am I the only one who feels like this, Master?
Or are all people locked within their being,
never fully expressing themselves
because of a barrier of restraint
or a fear of ridicule?

How good it is that I can talk to You, Lord.
When I am alone I can even speak out loud,
putting into words to You
what I cannot tell others.
You are my safety valve, the patient Listener,
and at the same time Helper and Guide.
How could I live without You?

# Self-acceptance

Lord, teach me self-acceptance!
Let me learn to take myself as I am
and not hanker after what I would be.
It seems a failing of human nature
that short people want to be tall
and tall ones try to hide their height.
Why can we never be satisfied?
This is a personal matter, Master,
but you know how I detest my nose . . .
It's just too long for my type of face.
It makes me miserable
for I feel folk are looking at it,
joking about it behind my back
and that makes me unhappy.

Oh dear! I realise, Master, what is happening.
I'm thinking about myself all the time,
self-centred, introspective, morose;
and in this mood quite unable to see
that everyone else is pre-occupied
with their own shortcomings
and not bothering about me.
How You must laugh at us, Lord!
As if a centimetre more or less on a nose
could affect a character or destiny,
unless it blinded its owner to the truth:
that what we are within is far more important
than our appearance.

So keep me sensible about myself, Lord,
even if I wish You had given me more handsome features.
Keep me from staring at myself in the mirror
with a longing, a sigh or a groan.
Let me get on with the urgent matter of living,
by accepting the framework You have provided for me.

# Rejection

Master, I feel worthless;
unloved, unwanted, brushed aside,
cheapened in my own eyes
and in the view of others.

How much of the blame is mine?
Some part, of course.
My tongue is too sharp and quick
for the comfort of those around me;
my sulky moods depress and chill my environment,
my seeming arrogance is really only a veneer
to cover inward insecurity.

Lord, I turn to You in desperate need.
I want to be accepted . . . and loved
but I only meet with rejection.
Can You save me from myself?
Can You make me into a new person
with different ways?
Can You break down the wall of my self-centredness
and make a window out to others?

O God . . . I'm at the end of my tether!
You must help me for no-one else can.

I place myself in Your hands.
I ask You to forgive all my sins and failings.
Create in me a clean heart
and let me make a new beginning,
looking up to You instead of inward to myself,
and claiming Your aid.

## This one day

This one day, Lord, is mine.
Your gift to me, fresh from Your hands;
heralded by the twittering of birds,
cleansed by the dawn wind,
warmed by the sun's first rays . . .
This day is mine!

This one shining day is my own.
I bless its early hours
as I commit it to You.
I yield myself into Your care
knowing I am secure in Your love,
whatever the coming hours may bring.

Please, Master, make it a good day,
filled with happy work-hours
and rewarding leisure,
a really-good-to-be-alive day.

Let today be a day I shall remember,
not because of some world-shaking event,
but because it was a golden day,
glowing with happiness.
Let it be a day of inward harmony and outward peace,
of joybells within
and laughter without;
a carefree rollicking kind of a day
when my heart spins its own thread of fun,
to weave a bright pattern through all that happens.

And when I lay my head on my pillow tonight,
let my heart be warm with gratitude to You
for all life's good gifts.
Let my last thought be a contented:
"Thank You, Lord."

# Poison

Poison comes in varied forms, Master,
    in many dangerous forms,
and never worse than when it masquerades
    as freedom of choice.

Has a baker freedom to put strychnine in his bread,
arguing that if people don't want it,
    they needn't buy it?
Can a factory spew out chemical waste
nonchalantly pointing out that those who don't approve
    should live elsewhere?
Yet the protagonists of licentious freedom
    advocate dirty films
    pornographic papers
    perverse photos
    dangerous drugs . . .
all in the name of liberty of choice,
    and freedom to experiment.

Freedom to experiment, Lord?
Must I become drunk to know the danger of alcohol?
Must I take poison to learn its power?
Shall I plunge into a smelly sewer
    to note the effect

or drug my brain to achieve weird sensations?
O God; this is freedom to damn oneself,
to destroy the marvellous body and mind You have
    created,
        to sully one's eternal soul
        with the filth of deadly sin.

Save me, Lord, from this kind of moral poison.
Keep me pure in mind and heart.
Wake me up to the perils of trying to see
how near I can go to the edge of the precipice
        without falling over.
O God! You must help me!

# LOVE AND MARRIAGE

# Is this love?

Lord, I *must* talk to You.
That young man I met yesterday bowled me over.
I've never felt like that before.
It seemed that an invisible cord drew us together
and when our eyes met, something magnetic happened.
        At least it did to me.
I thrilled, I responded with all my being;
        suddenly I was happy.

I wondered if he felt the same but I couldn't tell.
        A little later he had to leave
        and I felt such a vacuum.
Friends continued to chat
        but it meant nothing to me
        for my thoughts were elsewhere.

Is this real love, Master?
This sudden quickening of interest in a stranger,
this increase in the pulse's tempo?

Can it happen to one of two
        and not to the other?
Today I'm wondering.

What do I know of this young man except his name
        and that my heart responded to him at once?
Was it merely physical attraction,
        or a deeper call from the spirit?

Lord, it is a relief to open my heart to You
        for at this stage I can tell no other.
I don't want to make any mistake in this important matter
        of falling in love.
I can't control what I feel
        but I can control the expression of those feelings.
Do help me, Master. I need You urgently just now.

## Lover's tiff

It was all his fault, Lord!
He deliberately aggravated me
        when he knew I was feeling down.
He knows that I dislike that green tie
        so he wore it to annoy me,

and he called me 'kid'
        as though I wasn't grown up.
I'm simply seething with rage.

I admit that I flared up too quickly.
After a difficult day at work
        my nerves were on edge.
I needed soothing, not irritating;
I wanted him to take me in his arms
        telling me how much he loved me.
Instead of which he teased me. I blazed at him
        and flounced out of the room,
        telling him to go home.

I'm miserable, Master, near to tears,
        but it really was his fault,
        well, most of it;
        at least some of it.
I suppose I was touchy,
and perhaps he wasn't his best self.
I wonder if he'll phone to say he's sorry?
Perhaps I should phone first . . .
        but that would be hard to do.

Help me, Lord, to conquer my pride
        and forget my hurt.
It probably was mostly my fault . . .

Give me grace to say so and to take the blame.
It's hard, though . . .
Here goes, Master. *With Your help* I'll do it.
I'll call his number
and bring this lover's tiff to an end.

## Engaged

I'm engaged! But what does that mean?
A telephone can be 'engaged' one moment
and free the next,
but surely not a person, not a *real* person?
Lord, help me to realise what I have done.
I have plighted my troth, my love and loyalty,
to a fine young man.

Does he really want me to share his life?
This comparative stranger . . . how shall I live with him?
We don't really know each other in depth.
Oh, we know the outside, the way we look and dress,
the smiles, the loving glances.
We're on our best behaviour with each other as yet
but our fears and weaknesses, our shortcomings,
we keep locked within our own breasts.

We must break down these barriers before we marry;
talk freely to each other.
Will our love survive the ordeal of early breakfast
and the rush to work?
Will it outlast the off-moments that each one has,
nature's dark side showing through?
Will it last through sunshine and storm,
through youth and up to old age?

It must, Lord! It *will*, Master, with Your help.
As we take this step together we bow before You,
acknowledging our need of You.
Lay Your hand upon our heads,
You Who have given us the gift of mutual love,
Expand and deepen it,
so that the buffeting winds of life
will only serve to strengthen the roots
which bind us together.
Looking up into Your face, Master,
we believe we see Your approving smile.

# Wedding day

I'm excited and yet afraid, Lord.
Now my wedding day has dawned I hesitate
    and tremble . . .
It is such a momentous step to take
    into a mysterious veiled future.
Even now as I talk to You, Master,
the threads of the day's events are twining together
    in a pre-arranged pattern
to culminate in the high-spot of the ceremony.

Before I pledge myself to my husband,
I want to give myself once more to You.
I invite You, Lord, to be the first guest
    in our new home:
    invisible yet potently present,
    influencing all we say and do,
    guiding us in all our decisions.

I'm so glad that You chose to be present
    at the wedding in Cana of Galilee
    in Your days on earth, Master,
for it shows that You can share the highest joys,
    the fun and laughter,

bringing them a new element of happiness.
I might otherwise have thought of You too often
    as the Man of Sorrows,
and left You out of my planning
    for supreme moments of bliss.

Join with us, Lord, as we make our solemn vows,
and remain with us in the family fun that will follow.
May this be a day which we shall both remember
    as the happiest day of our life.
With Your blessing, it can be so.

# Everything new

It's a thrill, Master, all this newness around me:
    New clothes, new furniture, new carpets.
I could dance around my little home in happiness.
    And yet I am afraid . . .
afraid of spoiling all this pristine cleanness,
afraid of using the oven in case I stain it,
afraid of spilling on the gleaming carpet,
afraid of chipping one of the best cups.

Why should I feel afraid like this, Master?
    Alas, I know the answer.

All my life I have been painfully aware
 that freshness wears off.
That the simple fact of being used wears the surface away,
 gives things an older look.
Each time I have worn a new dress or shoes or coat,
 I have determined to keep them like new
 but it has been impossible.
Wear and tear show in some way.

I remind myself, though, that antiques command higher
 prices
 than newly acquired goods.
Perhaps I need that philosophy, Master,
 To use with care
so that these our possessions age gracefully.
I pray that for myself as well, Lord.
I too cannot escape the marks of living
 for in some way it will show
however hard I try to keep the wrinkles at bay.
Help me to mature with grace.

One thing I would ask, Master.
Let our new-found union, so filled with joy,
 never become casual and perfunctory.
Let it be refreshed and renewed day by day,
through the joy of Your presence in our lives.

# Aftermath

What a rush life can be, Lord!
I feel worn out with work and home duties
exhausting my strength
and straining my nerves.
I have been a bit bad-tempered lately, I admit,
but that is because of stress.
I thought married life would be easier
and I find it has its pitfalls.

Just the sharing of cupboards can be traumatic.
A woman needs a lot of room for her clothes,
an extra share of wardrobe space,
but somehow he can't see that, Master.
Then meals . . . he likes a hearty breakfast
and I am permanently slimming.
He likes coffee, I prefer tea,
but it is a bother to make both.
Why should I always have to give in to him?
Can people so different in their ways
learn to live in harmony,
without one capitulating to the other?

I love, admire and respect my husband
but we are *two people*, Lord!

When we united our lives,
we didn't merge our personalities.
I'm still me!
Help me, Lord, in this matter.
I want my marriage to succeed and last.
Help us both to seek a peaceful compromise
when opinions differ,
and let us work to achieve harmony between ourselves
and within the walls we are proud to call our home.

## The waiting time

Inwardly I rejoice, Lord. The doctor has confirmed it.
I can share this thrilling news with You, Master . . .
I'm expecting a baby.
This is Your gift, Your generous sharing with human parents
in the act of procreation.
A new person is being formed inside me,
unlike anyone else before.
It's a delightful secret in the family for the moment,
but soon it will be blazoned abroad.

I sit and muse, Lord.
I see myself wheeling a pram, changing nappies,
cuddling a toddler, praying over a cot.
It's a big responsibility that I hardly dare face,
so I'm relying on Your help, Lord.
To have a precious life entrusted to my care,
a child to train and guide,
to shape its destiny
by the way its first years are passed . . .
Oh make me worthy of this trust, Master.
Mistakes I shall surely make, but may they be few
with no lasting consequences.

Help me to prepare myself during the waiting time,
not only physically but spiritually.
Let me live in harmony with myself and others,
casting out every anxiety,
imbibing peace and joy and love from Your bounteous supply,
and centering my thoughts upon Your constant care
for me and my child.
Thank You, Lord, that I can count on You.

# Still waiting

I'm tired of it, Master.
Nine whole months is too long!
The days are beginning to drag . . . I'm heavy,
heavy in body and spirit.
Today in exasperation I hid away the baby-cot;
I couldn't bear its teasing emptiness any longer.
"This child will never come," I affirmed.
"Did you ever hear of a pregnant woman
who didn't finally give birth?"
my husband enquired soothingly.
"No!" I stormed, "but someone's got to be first."
He asked: "Why do you stick yourself out in front like
that
when you walk?"
and I retorted: "So as not to fall on my nose."
He thinks I'm trying to draw attention to my happy
condition
but I'm just doing a balancing act.

Lord, grant me patience,
patience to wait my time,
which is Your time.

I seem to be dulled by waiting,
    dull and heavy, heavy and dull.
I didn't expect it to be like this;
I thought I should be starry-eyed to the finish,
    but it's long, Lord, so long . . .
I got everything ready too soon, much too soon,
    for I was eager, thrilled and involved.
I'm not good at waiting, Master!
Let me hold Your hand as my time draws near,
and as day succeeds uneventful day, let me say:
    "I'm one step nearer journey's end."

## My baby

This morning a small bundle was laid in my arms,
my first-born child, a gift from You, Lord.
So that is what I waited nine months to see?
    That red and wrinkled face,
    those exquisite miniature hands,
    so perfect, so complete in detail.
I feel maternally possessive. It's *my* baby,
    part of my very physical self.
I can understand the fury of a tigress
    when defending her young.
I too would risk my life
    to save my child from harm.

I love the word-picture in the gospels,
where You took small children in Your arms
and blessed them.
It shows another side of You;
not only Lord, Master, Healer and Leader,
but a young man with a love for little ones.

May I bring my new baby to You today, Lord?
In thought I come slowly forward,
the precious child hugged tightly in my arms,
searching Your face for a sign of acceptance.
Your eyes smile a welcome as I lay my treasure
in Your outstretched hands.
Time stands still as You bless him,
then You hand him back to me.
I won't forget, Lord. He's my child,
but he's Yours too, now.
Oh guide me in his upbringing,
so that we both can have joy in him.

# LESSONS TO LEARN

# The blind man

Thank You, Lord, for the words exchanged
    and the exhilaration they brought me.
The heavy traffic rumbled past,
    filling our nostrils with petrol fumes
as we patiently queued at the bus stop.
Alerted by his white stick
    I entered into conversation.

"Wasn't the traffic noisy?", was my first venture,
but he countered it with a nonchalant:
    "I don't notice it.
I fix my mind on other things,
green fields, flowers and leafy trees.
In that way I escape the present.
It's a good solution," he chuckled.

And that was a blind man's reaction
    to a tiring and long wait.

I realised I was in the presence
of a philosopher of great worth.
What a lesson he taught me!
What insight he gave me into the secret
of a serene mind.
There was I, with all my senses unblunted,
feeling aggrieved at having to wait;
whereas a sightless man could point the way
to inner harmony.

We boarded the bus and sat together,
continuing our conversation.
When I left him I thanked him sincerely
for having given my spirit a lift.
Master! at times I grumble at much smaller set-backs
than the loss of sight.
Help me to learn the blind man's secret of living
with inner resources ever at hand.

# The 'I know' people

Lord, deliver me from the 'I know' people!
"I know what you want . . .
I know how you feel . . .
I know what you should do . . ."

Master, they don't know!
How can they?
They are not me, in my circumstances,
with my temperament and talents . . . and failings.

That man in the shop.
I can still see his triumphant smile:
"I've got exactly what you want."
He hadn't!
He hadn't even grasped what I was seeking.

The woman in the bus:
"I know how you feel . . ."
A rainy morning, a heavy cold, tired feet,
Yes, there were all those ingredients,
but what did she know of the letter I'd received:
the crushing of hopes,
anxiety for a loved one,
happy plans now spoiled?

Lord, give me patience with the 'I know' people.
Let me recognise their goodwill
and would-be helpfulness,
and let me express my gratitude
at least with a generous smile
and a pleasant word.

# Coals of fire

Live coals of fire,
glowing, hot and searing,
which I would pour on to my enemy's head.
I breathe them out upon him now
for I am blazing with wrath,
exploding in anger against him.

But, Master, I know that's hardly what Your Book means
when it counsels us to pour coals of fire
upon our enemies.
You would have us love them!
Can love ever be like a devouring fire
which scorches and hurts and maims,
even consumes its object?
I know the answer to that.

Then what kind of coals of fire can I heap upon
those who oppose me?
If it is to be fire, it must be something which warms,
heartens, comforts, brightens,
and the name of that fire is love.
Love expressed in a kind word, a helpful action,
a friendly attitude,
a cheery smile.

By attacking my enemy I cause him to strengthen
his position.
By conciliation I weaken his defences
and enter by a backdoor
in the hope of agreement and concord.

I will not deny, Lord, that at times
I had far rather burn my enemy than love him,
but help me to go Your way, to try Your remedy,
for patching up the quarrels
seemingly inherent in human relationships.

# Gales

I'm frightened, Lord, of high winds
when the sky darkens,
the windows rattle
and the garden fence sways ominously.
There is something sinister about the unleashed
forces of nature.
At first there is a brooding stillness:
all nature sulking in a sombre hush
of dark foreboding.

## TOWARDS YOU, LORD

I note the dull steel colour of the clouds
which herald the approaching storm
and my heart sinks.

The wind rises and in a few moments the trees
are bowed before its power,
leaves revealing their pale undersides
like the fluttering of women's petticoats.
The tall masts of the pines sway wisely,
(better to cede a point than to snap)
while the crash of dead branches accompanies the tinkling
of tiles falling from the roof.

The heavy rain pelts down and soon a watery sun appears,
splitting the jagged clouds
and girding them with gold.
My mind lifts vigorously to You, Lord.
Help me, Master, when the gales of life buffet me,
when everything of value seems at risk.
Teach me, like the pines, to bend but not break,
to be strong yet pliable
and to live on in hope.

# Laying down one's life

The monument, Master, made me think.
It commemorated the death of young men for their
country.
But, Lord, I can think of other ways,
less glorious, less renowned,
but no less demanding,
of laying down one's life for others.

There is the mother with a mentally retarded
or handicapped child,
which she devotedly tends day and night;
the daughter caring for her frail parents
through years of personal self-denial;
the single parents struggling alone against many odds
to rear a young family.
All these are giving blood, sweat and tears
to accomplish what they feel to be their duty.

No memorial will ever be erected to them,
no laurel wreath be engraved over their names,
yet they too have made a supreme sacrifice,
giving their life blood slowly, drop by drop.

Surely an equally heroic sacrifice,
though often unseen and unsung.
But Your eyes, Lord, take note and their self-giving
is precious in Your sight.

Come to such as these just now with a thought of courage,
an uplift of heart,
a remembrance of joy.
I pray for them, Master, not knowing their names,
but understanding something of their great need.
These unknown heroes and heroines, these noble souls . . .
Make them equal, Lord, to the burden they so willingly
take
upon their hearts and shoulders.
Grant them a sense of Your presence today.

## Sunny Bank

My heart thrilled with pleasure, Lord,
as I read the name Sunny Bank.
Thank You for that, Master.
I felt it was Your gift to me
on that dull wet morning,

I sat in a bus on a shopping trip when the roadname
caught my eye, Sunny Bank!

My mind fought against reality,
that a road with that delightful name could be
merely a viaduct over a railway,
drab, grey and noisy.

I clung to the picture the name conjured up . . .
In thought I saw children gathering primroses in spring,
pouncing eagerly upon the gay flowers
in the hedgerows;
couples strolling along the narrow path
by the railway siding,
while a leisurely engine puffed slowly past;
families picnicking in the lush grass,
yielding themselves outstretched to the sun's
pleasant warmth.
Pictures from the past when the name Sunny Bank
had been rightly given.
Was it not better, Lord, that I should dwell on those
than on the unpleasing present?

Isn't that Your gift, Master?
Your wondrous glowing gift,
that by imagination we can escape the present
to live in a fairyland of fantasy
for a few brief moments?
My heart felt warmed and happy
and the world seemed a better place.
Thank You, Lord, for Sunny Bank.

# Winter morning

There was washing to do, Master,
    but I didn't feel like it.
    Anyway, it wasn't urgent.
I wandered out to the garden
    into the chill raw air
in the hope of finding some early buds.

My startled gaze fell on some periwinkles,
    both white and blue.
It didn't seem long since I had planted them,
hardly long enough for them to flower.
Then the grass took my attention, not the grass
    where it should be, in the lawn,
but the flourishing tufts in the flower-beds.

I fetched a hoe and started to work.
Suddenly I realised that some birds were chirping,
    hidden from me in nearby trees.
Their song was one of mirth and gaiety,
certainly not reflecting the poor weather.

With lighter heart I plied my task
    then after half an hour I gave up,
    not tired but invigorated.

I marched indoors and soon had the washing machine
purring,
then I cleaned the kitchen and did some cooking,
feeling jubilant with my progress.
What delightful surprises You had in reserve for me,
Lord,
on that dull winter morning.
Thank You!

# Mountain and plain

The view was glorious, Lord!
From the mountain top I could see other ranges,
stretching away into misty horizons.
There in the valley lay a tiny toy town
of miniature houses and cars,
unbelievably small.
Up on the heights the sun warmed
despite the surrounding snow
which glistened diamond white.
The deep blue sky domed far above enclosing
pure exhilarating air.
I felt liberated, joyful, near to You, Master,
with You near to me.

Then the heights challenged me!
As I looked down to the diminutive town
I felt my own frustrations and irritations shrink.
In the clear mountain air I summoned fresh courage.
"Never again," I cried, "will I be petty or mean."
But I have been just that, Master!
Back on the plain, people and problems loomed big
and the mountain experience seemed far away,
        unreal and impossible,
quite meaningless in a workaday world.

Forgive me, Lord!
Forgive my human frailty, that spiritual visions
        evaporate with change of circumstance,
that high resolves vanish when stress returns.
Don't let me lose the enlarged vision,
        even if I can't realise it.
Let it be an aim, an ideal,
that will raise my life above my lowest endeavours.

# SPIRITUAL STOCKTAKING

# Waste products

I realise, Master, that my life is cluttered,
littered with waste products
that do no good to anyone,
impeding my progress.
Help me to get rid of them, Lord.
First I would mention anxiety;
what a worrier I am!
I can build the proverbial molehill
not only into a mountain,
formidable and impassable,
but into a range of high Alps.
Help me to cease worrying over what I can't alter,
and to take some action in events I can influence.
That will be one waste product less in my life.

Then there is resentment, Master.
I'm ashamed of the stiff antipathy I sense
to some people and their ways.

So much energy goes into these feelings
that I am drained and nervy afterwards.
Help me to banish resentment from my nature,
knowing that the events which call it forth
are not worth the emotion expended on them.

Then there are regrets.
        "If only I had done this . . . or that."
I go over the circumstances in my mind,
        chiding myself, blaming myself,
but the incident is in the past
        and cannot be erased.
        Regrets are useless.
It will only be with Your help, Lord,
that these ugly waste products can be cleared away,
but what a pleasant atmosphere they will leave behind.

# Quick results

We live in quick-result days, Master.
Desirable goods can be obtained
        by pressing a button,
        opening a tin
        or defrosting a packet.

As long as one can pay, one can obtain
 instant satisfaction.

Suntan without sun is promised
by the simple application of a cream or spray.
You lie down marked with winter's pallor
to arise as from a holiday on a sunny beach,
 glowingly, faultlessly, tanned all over.

We are spoiled, Lord, by this ability to take quick cuts,
 to pay in money
 rather than in effort;
to achieve easy counterfeits which look
 like the real thing.
But that is not possible with spiritual values.
There are no short cuts to holiness of life,
no funiculars up the mountain of Christian character.
It is easy to *look* good, simple to *sound* good,
quite possible to *feel* good, without *being* good.

O God, help me to be the real thing!
Clear out the subterfuges in my life.
 Let me be sincere and open,
not pretending to be more than I am
 or other than I am,
yet steadily progressing along the Christian pathway.

# Authority

Master, You spoke with authority . . .
How I would have liked to hear You!
It was not the authority of the drill sergeant
barking out orders to quaking recruits,
nor the authority of a strident voice raised above others
in heated debate.
It was never the authority of class distinction,
the upper addressing the lower,
and certainly not of age addressing youth.

What was the secret of Your authority, Lord?
I believe it was Your constant contact
with Your heavenly Father,
the seal of His approval on Your life;
the long prayer sessions on the mountain side
away from all distractions.
It must have been the certainty of Your calling,
total dedication to Your mission,
the authority of outgoing love
ignoring the cost of caring.
All these gave a backing, a build-up, a power,
to Your words.

Master, I want my life to ring true,
so that what I say
is not belied by what I do.
May there be a sincerity, a wholeness, an integrity
that will stamp me
as one of Your followers wherever I am
and whatever I do.

# My shadow

I'm uneasy about my shadow, Lord.
Not the shadow cast by light,
but the invisible shadow which is my influence.
Wherever I go this silent presence creeps after me,
mingles with my friends when we converse,
yet still flits around when I am silent.
It is short, touching those closest to me,
yet long, oh so long,
stretching right into the distance,
affecting known and unknown people . . .
and I can't control its action.

That is a serious thought, Lord.

I can never say: "Today I will exert a good influence."
    My shadow would mock me.
    It has a life of its own,
linked and dependent on mine, it is true,
yet far freer, mobile and self-determining.

The aura of what I am pervades
    what I do and say.
It sometimes nullifies my best endeavours,
    sets at nought my well-laid plans,
    puts obstacles in my way
and shouts aloud when I command silence.

What can I do, Master,
about this shadow which is my influence on others?
Will You so dwell within me in the fullness
    of Your Spirit,
that my life is under Your control?
Then I need not fear the effect
of my invisible shadow falling on others.

# Tongue ache

Wouldn't it be a good thing, Master,
        if we got tongue ache
when we had misused the gift of speech?
Or if a painful rash spread round the mouth
        when we had told lies
        or uttered cruel slander?
It would at least convince us that we had sinned.
        We get away with so much!
A smile on the face can accompany poisonous words,
        and with a nonchalant air
we can fire a loaded sentence into someone's mind,
starting off a trail of innuendo and suspicion.

Why are we so cruel with our words, Lord,
when we regard ourselves as kind in other ways?
Spiteful words are often lightly said,
        or harsh criticism given,
but what searing wounds, what painful scars, they leave;
breaking up friendships, sowing discord,
creating cliques and rivalries,
often forgotten by the one who spoke them
to live on in destructive power in the hearer.

Forgive the many times I have sinned with my words
and even if my tongue does not ache,
stab my conscience deeply enough to hurt
when I offend in speech.
Control my tongue, Master, 'keep the door of my lips.'
Let Your Spirit stand sentry-guard over my utterances.
Cleanse my inner being,
so that from its source only good and helpful words
will flow.

# Inflation

Lord, inflation seems to rule our lives.
We hear of it, discuss it and endure it daily,
but little is said of self-inflation
from which most of us suffer.

The blown-up me, a bloated balloony being,
filled with empty conceit and self-adulation:
other people don't see this aura of mine,
this imaginary extension of my personality,
so they bump into it
and I get hurt.
They prick my pride and I collapse,
furious and deflated for a time.

Then I'm there again, puffed up with a fresh injection
        of self-esteem;
swaggering around as though I owned the world
and expecting others to acclaim me.

Lord, deflation is a painful process
        but I know it is necessary.
As I come into Your presence
        and look up into Your face,
give me, I pray, such a sense of Your majesty,
        such a vision of Your greatness,
that I shall shrink to right proportions
        in my own eyes.
(In fact, it would do me good to appear even smaller)
        Then keep me there, Lord,
        keep me humble;
save me from the snare of self-inflation.

# Independence

It's wrong, Master,
I see now that it's wrong,
although all my life I have believed it right.
        I'm too independent!

It can be a kind of pride,
this spirit of 'I can manage on my own.'
It is not the worthy quality it would at first seem.

I ought to have accepted the lady's aid.
She only wanted to help me
and my cursed independence stood in the way.
Politely, oh so politely, I declined her assistance,
and went on my way bulging with self-satisfied esteem.
Then it struck me,
it hit me really hard, Lord,
that what I had considered a virtue was a failing
of serious dimension.
I was ready to give help but I couldn't accept it,
not gratefully and graciously.
My pride had erected a barrier of self-sufficiency,
and that pride was a form of sin.

Help me, Master!
To You I am willing to turn when I stand in need.
Then why can't I accept the kindnesses
that other people offer me?
Help me to smash this wall of self-sufficing
and to be more responsive to the efforts of others
to help me along life's path.

# Criticism

Criticism is unpleasant, Lord.
    It is bitter medicine,
administered often by a careless hand,
and it can smart and sting long after.
Why is it that all criticism seems unjustified?
Is it because we feel affronted when our
    personal territory is invaded?
We are like an indignant bird,
    angrily defending our garden path
    with squawks and fluttering wings;
or like a wild animal circling its domain
    with surly mien and warning growls.
Criticism we see as an enemy to be kept at bay.
    After all, we know best!

There's the rub, Master!
We see from within, others see from without
    and therefore opinions differ.
Where can the truth lie, Lord? Somewhere in between?
Can I never be right because I see everything
    from my own angle?
And are others always wrong when they see the matter
    from theirs?

Master, help me not to flare up when criticised.
Help me to search for the grain of truth
hidden in the unpalatable words,
making up my mind to profit by it,
and to throw away the rough chaff in which it was embedded.
Then even my enemies will be doing me a good turn, Lord,
by showing me where I can improve,
and that is something to be grateful for.

# TOWARDS YOU, LORD

# Towards You, Lord

I saw them this morning, Master,
tightly clenched praying hands,
lifted in mute worship to a Creator-God.
They were only the newborn leaves of a row of seedlings
still wrinkled and twisted;
but their fervent stretching into the unknown upper world
touched me deeply.

They were obeying an inner urge, bewildered yet joyful,
after having pierced earth's crust:
reaching timorously but strongly upward not knowing
how far they must go
before nature said enough.
Not knowing the storms of rain and wind they would meet,
the attacks of enemies unknown;
disobeying the law of gravity to fulfil their destiny
by obeying the higher law of growth.

Hearing nature's call to rise out of seeming death
to pulsing life, rising sap,
growth and expansion;
to the final revelation of the hidden bud and seed.

So may I, Lord, respond to that call from You
which disturbs my heart,
making me dissatisfied with earthly things,
with finite aims,
and filling me with longings inexpressible
for something beyond,
something to which You challenge me.
Grant me the pluck to do as the seedlings did,
to dare to answer,
confident, believing,
to stretch my hands upward, towards You, Lord.

# Hang-on faith

Lord, grant me faith, faith in You,
in Your purposes,
in Your wisdom and Your power,
but above all, in Your love.
I would have faith as a resplendent lamp,
glowing in darkness, lighting my path.

I would have faith as an endless treasure,
    from which to draw for daily needs.
I would have faith for total commitment to You,
    to live daily in childlike unconcern.
But, Master, my faith is only a grim hang-on faith,
    battered and worn by many conflicts,
    gripped tightly in my clutching fingers.
I dare not let it go, and yet it is so small!

It is my link with You, my vital link with You.
If I lose it, the gloom of doubt will close in upon me,
    the darkness of despair will cloud my steps.
I must hold fast to it, my tiny scrap of faith.
Sometimes I think I have lost it,
then a word from Your Book, a comment from a friend,
    or a line from a well-known hymn,
revives the near-extinguished flame.

I can't tell people how near I am to unbelief,
how cold doubt chills me until I almost give up,
how what I once accepted as true seems at times
    as empty fable and false hope.
But to You, Master, I confess my doubts as I pray:
    "Help my unbelief."
Yet through it all, in my hard-clenched fist,
I shelter this spark of faith left to me,
    this hang-on faith.
May it never be wrested from my grasp.

# It costs to care

It costs to care, Master!
You know that well Yourself...
Your love made You vulnerable to misunderstandings
among Your followers,
brought You contempt, opposition and hatred
from religious leaders,
and led You to a cross and a painful death.

Even I know that it costs to care, Lord.
Every tie of love with another creates a tender area
where a blow might fall.
To enlarge the circle of one's family, to increase
the number of one's friends,
is to offer oneself to possible bruising of spirit.

It hurts to love!
It is easier to close in upon oneself
and shut others out;
and yet I pray, O Lord,
expand my heart to embrace more people,
although it might cause pain;
widen the narrow channels of my love, so choked
with debris of my own concerns.

Let Your surging power sweep through, cleansing,
deepening and broadening my affections,
until I am more capable of loving, and therefore
more capable of suffering,
until I know the high cost of caring.

It is the way of the cross, Master,
the way You went.
Help me to follow in Your steps.

# Rebellion

Forgive me, Lord! I didn't trust You.
I thought You had let me down,
that You didn't care;
perhaps hadn't heard my prayer,
or had just ignored it as unimportant.
Yet it was important to me,
vital, I felt.
I saw only the one solution and prayed desperately
for its realisation,
only to be frustrated.

Master, I felt bitter against You!

It wasn't much that I asked and it didn't affect
        other people, but only me.
Why could it not be granted?

Then as the days passed, I saw why.
You had something better in store for me,
something for which I have thanked You
        a hundred times at least.
I'm so ashamed, Master, of my temporary rebellion
        against Your way for me;
You were planning in the shadows
        while I demanded the light of day.

Help me to learn a lesson, Lord,
        to trust You,
        trust Your love and caring,
even when my own plans are set aside
        and my own hopes thwarted.

# Saints

You want to make us saints, Master?
Isn't that rather a barren hope,
a pinnacle of achievement too far away in the clouds
        to be feasible?

Me, a saint?
with my temperament, my weaknesses, failings
    and contradictions?
You're joking, Lord!
You know the ingredients of my personality,
all I have inherited from my forbears of good
    and less good
and to be quite frank, of evil.

You set the standard too high, Lord,
and You won't leave me in peace.
    You pull and push,
    nudge and prod,
You prune and discipline and train
to raise me to a higher spiritual level,
and I am like a recalcitrant donkey, kicking,
    plunging and resisting.

Why do You continue to bother with me?
Honestly, Master, the heights of holiness do call me,
I feel their attraction, their challenge,
    but I am way down in the valley
    and the snowy heights are distant.
Don't despair of me, Master.
Don't yield to my obstinacy and leave me alone.
Keep working at me, believing for me,
    leading me upwards.

Don't get a halo ready for me just yet,
    for it wouldn't fit.
Let me struggle and endure and aspire,
and one day I pray I may win through.

## Progress

Progress is a funny business, Lord.
It is often one step forward,
    then a slide back again.
One invention cancels out another,
and every new item produced creates a desire
    for something else,
a desire which becomes a need, a burning need.

What irony that when washing machines
    became customary in most homes,
new textiles were produced that required hand-wash.
No sooner were thermostatic irons popular
    than no-iron fabrics appeared.
Following the acquisition of a spin-drier,
    one resents the label: 'Do not spin'
    on the new purchases.

We are kept in a perpetual state of expecting
something different, beyond the present,
and yet we are left unsatisfied.

Spiritual progress is otherwise, Lord,
for You are in charge there.
You are not always thinking how to outwit us,
hoodwink us into trying new ways.
Spiritual progress is slow, even unnoticeable
by the person concerned,
and only You can assess the ground covered
and the improvement made.
Perhaps our greatest step forward is when we see ourselves
as we are in Your sight,
which can be a very unnerving experience.
Our greatest comfort is that we are in Your hands,
and You know the goal to which You are leading us.
Help us to plod on faithfully.

## Living with mistakes

It's hardly fair, Master,
that we only live life once through,
so that we rarely profit by our own mistakes

and in obdurate blindness fail to learn
from others' mishaps..
Sometimes, then, we have to live with our mistakes,
things we have done or not done
which have brought consequences that now
hedge us in
or bar progress in a certain direction.

We blame ourselves, we grit our teeth,
all to no avail.
Give us courage, Master, to turn over
the blotted page,
to regard the mistake as a lesson to learn,
an experience dearly paid for
and therefore valuable.

If only time were a clock that could be put back
a few days or months,
so that being given a second chance we could act
more wisely!
But no, Master, that is wishful thinking.
One must learn to live with one's mistakes,
reaping the harvest of ill-conceived plans,
or regretting a missed opportunity.

I dare to believe, Lord, that You can weave
even our shortcomings into an acceptable pattern;
perhaps not Your ideal will for our lives

but still something of value to Your Kingdom on earth.
To that encouraging thought I cling.
I beg You, Master, to build even my mistakes
into something worthwhile and to Your glory.

# HOSPITAL INTERLUDE

# Why me?

Why me, Lord?
Why should this happen to me?
What have I done to deserve it?
A serious illness . . . possibly an operation,
    I can't face it!
What law of health have I broken?
I've tried to follow sensible rules of living,
    to give my body what it needs
to function as the intricate machine it is.
Then why should illness overtake me?

I know I've been tense and worried lately,
    with daily problems almost crushing me,
but Master, life is complicated in our times,
vastly more so than when You strode the earth.
Yet I remember there were sick people then,
    lining the roads as You passed . . .
waiting to see You, hear You, touch You
    and receive healing from You.

Is disease part of our mortal heritage,
    part of our alienation from God?
Is it a price we pay as part of the human family
where pollution of air and water can slowly kill
    and chemicals abound in pre-packed food?

Help me not to complain, Master,
    at what has befallen me.
Sickness has struck my mortal body
    but it can't damage my immortal soul,
unless I allow it to build a wall of partition
    between You and me.
This can be an experience which lifts me nearer You,
    my weakness relying on Your strength.
Stay by me, Lord, and see me through, I plead.

## One in a row

My heart is at zero-point, Lord,
    and my spirits are flagging.
I feel desperately alone yet that is just
    what I am not.
I am one in a row of bed-patients.

## HOSPITAL INTERLUDE

"This is your bed," said the nurse kindly,
and I climbed into it with leaden feet.
    *My* bed? For how long?
A frightening prospect of uncounted days
    looms before me.
I lie in total isolation of spirit,
    not alone yet lonely,
with that desperate loneliness which seeps
    into every cell of the body,
    and chills the mind.

From the fortress of my bed,
the only spot which is mine for the time being,
    I survey the scene.
The business of the ward continues,
    voices, laughter, footsteps,
    trolley-wheels passing,
all of them a curtain shutting me in upon myself.
Master, I cling to You now in wordless prayer.
    Take away my fear, quiet my spirit,
let me burst out of this well of misery within
    to find what is positive and good.

The patients on each side of me smile a greeting.
Shall I be as calm as they when I have settled in?
    O help me, Lord! I trust in You.
You are with me here just as in my own home.

Let me believe it, even if I do not feel it.
        Let me rest in Your love,
even when I cannot frame a prayer.

## Under observation

Cold panic grips me, Master, and I shudder,
here between the sheets of this well-made bed,
too impersonal for my liking.
After a brief farewell my loved one went,
leaving me in hospital 'for observation'.
        The very words chill me . . .
I have a feeling of eyes watching me,
        invisible eyes hidden in the ceiling,
stealthy eyes peering from under beds.
        'Under observation' . . .
The doctors are kind and competent,
        the nurses cheery and helpful,
        the other patients sympathetic,
but I feel so alone, so helpless, so anxious
        about the future.

I wipe away a silent tear.
You must forgive me for crying, Lord.

I don't usually give way like this.
Help me to be brave.
A quiet thought comes to me bringing courage,
bringing comfort.
I'm under observation, under *Your* observation, Master,
You know where I am, You know all about me;
Your loving glance rests upon me in compassion,
Your all-seeing eye spies out my distress.
You know what lies before me, ere even the doctors
find out.
I'm not alone. I'm not abandoned,
I'm in Your loving care.

Thank You, Master. My tears have dried
and I lift my heart to You in childlike confidence,
knowing that I am under Your observation
and in Your will.

# Visitors

The clock hand creeps on, Lord,
and soon it will be visiting time.
The nurses have given a final tweak to the bedspreads
so that we all look spruce and tidy

and soon the ward doors will open
        and the eager visitors advance.
Some know their way and make straight for the right bed,
while others search the patients' faces
        for well-known features,
until a smile of recognition unites them.

It is good to see someone you love,
        to hear the home news
        and tell your own tale of woe.
Good to have someone sitting there for a time,
        just to see you, hear you, visit you.
It makes you feel so special, so precious, so wanted.

Time is up! So quickly?
A close handclasp, a kiss, a word of prayer
        and the loved one has gone.
There is a blank feeling, a momentary depression,
then the mind begins to recapture the conversation,
savouring again the snippets of news,
        and reliving happy moments.

Thank You, Lord, for human bonds of love
        between kinsfolk and friends,
        this echo of Your divine love
which warms and comforts and cheers.
And when the visitors have gone,
        You, the faithful Friend, remain,

spreading Your own rich love like a warm benediction.
    Thank You, Lord.

# Pain

Pain is hard to bear, Master,
even the dulled pain following sedation.
It stifles thought and smothers desire,
draining one of all but the longing to be free
    from its tyranny.
Help me to bear pain bravely, Lord,
    without feeling sorry for myself
    or envious of others less afflicted;
without venting my strained nerves on those around me.

Pain can teach me many lessons, Master.
It links me with suffering humanity all round the world,
levelling all classes, shades of colour and nationalities.
The groan of pain is the same in all languages,
    it unites us all.
It is nature's warning that something is wrong,
    and in that sense is invaluable,
but to be in constant pain, unalleviated,
is to be reduced in human potential.

I do not ask to escape pain, Lord, but I ask
to be able to bear my share of it
when it is inevitable,
without feeling that You have forsaken me,
or ceased to care for me.
Let pain be Your messenger to my heart.
Not a welcome one, certainly,
but one that can teach a lesson of endurance,
of compassion for others,
and of my great dependence upon You,
and Your hourly help.

## A new perspective

Lord, I am ashamed of myself!
Here in this hospital bed, I have made a discovery
which I hope will influence my whole life.
I came in here filled with self-pity:
my illness, my pain, my treatment,
created the bounds of my horizon.
Unknowingly I had become self-obsessed, self-centred,
with the spokes radiating out
to further spheres of self-interest.

## HOSPITAL INTERLUDE

Here a new perspective has been granted me,
    and for that I thank You, Master.
When the patient in the next bed told me her story
    — five operations in as many years —
and yet spoke hopefully and uncomplainingly,
    I felt like a worm.
It hit me hard to think how big a song I had made
    about my own troubles.
As I learned of others in the ward
    in far worse plight than I,
I began to see that my own burdens were light
    compared with many there.

That is something gained from this illness, Master,
    a better sense of perspective in life,
    a lessening of the 'me-mine' syndrome.
Grant that I do not forget this experience
    when I return home,
    cured of my illness, I hope,
    but also of my self-interest.

# Nightfall

The day nurses have gone
and a quieter tempo reigns.
Sister comes round with her pills and potions
    and patients settle for the night.
It is early by normal standards,
    but bedtime by hospital routine.
Nightfall is rather depressing, Master,
    for it brings more time to think.
The bustle of the day programme is over,
no more trolleys, tea-wagons or visits,
    the night hours lie ahead.

First in the silence I lift my heart to You, my Lord.
    I pray for myself,
    my needs, hopes and longings,
then I commit my loved ones to Your care.
    Sleep does not come easily . . .
there is a restless stirring from nearby beds,
revealing that others cannot settle at once.
In the semi-darkness each is a prey to thoughts
that can better be kept at bay in the daytime.

Friend of mine, O loving Lord,
Thank You that I can turn to You,

pouring out in silent monologue all that fills my heart.
How can people live without You?
How can they face the storms of life without the anchor
of a supporting faith?
To me it is unthinkable as I yield myself in confidence
to Your unsleeping care
until day dawns
and the busy life of the hospital ward begins again.

## Healing

O Christ, divine Healer, I would meet with You
for my need is great.
My body is sick and I long to be well.
I am weary of the pain, the weakness, the depression,
that seem to shadow my days.
I can't summon up the energy to pray
but I will try to place myself in Your presence.

Master, You who walked the dusty roads of this earth
in human form,
You know the limitations of the body.
You experienced hunger, thirst and weariness,
yes, wracking pain and ebbing life.

## TOWARDS YOU, LORD

In my thoughts I come to You as though I met You
        at some village well.
You sit there alone as I approach
        and You greet me with a smile.

Soon I am telling You all about myself,
although I judge You know already.
It is a relief to tell You how I feel,
        You have the patience to listen.
I pour it all out, the physical troubles first,
then haltingly my frustrations and set-backs,
        jangling quarrels,
        deep disillusions . . .
What a shattered life I am laying bare before You!

Stretch out Your hand, Master,
Lay it on my head and let me hear: "Peace, be still,"
        so that my racing thoughts are quieted.
Then speak the word of forgiveness,
so that I may be released from inward tension.
Finally, as I dare to look into Your face,
let me hear You say: "Be whole!"

# Glad news

Hurray, Lord! Tomorrow I go home!
It's delightful news and I'm thrilled.
I've told my dear one what clothes to bring.
        Will they still fit me?
Let me see, how long have I been here?

I'm a bit nervous though, Lord,
nervous about whether I shall be able to cope;
a bit afraid of testing my own strength
        against the demands of everyday life.
I've been spoiled in hospital . . .
        meals served to the minute,
        clean sheets on the bed
without any thought of laundry matters,
the competent nurses and bustling helpers,
the camaraderie of the other patients . . .
        I shall miss it all, I know,
but it will be great to be in my own home again,
        however small it may appear
to my hospital-widened eyes.

Thank You, Master, for Your help in the day of trouble.
Thank You for the healing which has come
        through the good care given me.

Now on my last evening in the ward,
I commit my life into Your hands once again,
asking Your blessing on the morrow,
as I return home.
May I have gained something from my hospital sojourn;
may I be a wiser, better, stronger person, with Your aid.

# BEREFT

# Bereft

It's happened to me, Master,
that heaviest blow to a marriage,
 the death of the beloved partner.
When we made our life-long vows we knew it was
 "till death us part,"
but that moment seemed eons away in a misty future.
Now my turn has come to walk alone.
 I'm glad my loved one went first,
glad that I could tend and serve him to his last day.
 Thank You, Lord, for that.

Now I'm one of the great host of those who face single
  life
 after years of intimate comradeship.
I accept my lot without complaint
 for I am but one among many.
I have loved and been loved,
now I must meet life's challenges alone.

Master, it is not easy!
There is a painful shrinking from assuming burdens,
a desperate need to confide in someone,
    to share with another.
For a time it seems a half-life,
    a mechanical doing of duties,
    a painful remembering,
but Your presence relieves some of the sting
and gives hope for the days ahead.

One day there will be a re-union in that Beyond
    which You have prepared.
So help me, Lord, to live worthily,
making of each day something of value.

# Heartache

Heartache is a very real thing, Master,
a continuous pressure on the emotions
    that leaves one drained and weary.
Physical pain would be easier to bear
    for some remedy could be applied,
but this gnawing at the vitals of one's being
    knows no alleviation.

## BEREFT

This inward hurting is hard to endure.
    Part of me has been wrenched away
and the wound is open, gaping open, Master,
yet I must hide it from others' eyes,
    for they would not understand.
Folk are kind to me and thoughtful, Lord,
    and I am grateful.
They remind me of all life still holds for me.
    I know their words are true
yet there is a revulsion of feeling within me
as though I must refuse to be comforted,
    at any rate for the time being.

Does time heal, Master? It is said that it does
    and I expect it is true,
but I crave more than that thought just now.
I want to feel Your loving arms around me,
I want to hear You say: "Be comforted.
    Your loved one is with me."
The warmth of Your presence will bring
    soothing balm.
Your loving care will wrap a tender mantle around me
    until my wounds are healed
    and my heartache assuaged.
Come to me just now, my Lord.

# Stabs of Remembrance

It's the little things, Master, that hurt most.
Stabs of remembrance pierce my heart
        over such tiny trifles,
        linked with a loved one
gone on the long journey from which no-one returns.
That link gives them power to move me deeply.

An empty arm-chair shouts its disuse,
a well-worn purse brings a lump to my throat,
        a marking in a favourite book,
        an underlined text in the Bible
        or a cross against a chosen hymn,
all speak in potent language to my sensitive heart.

These swift stabs of remembrance bring pain, Lord,
        yet thankful, grateful pain,
        happy memories misted with sorrow,
a veil of regret thin enough to allow some of the light
        to shine through,
stings of memory glowing with warm feeling.
For these things only hurt because a love-relationship
        has been broken,
otherwise I should be indifferent to them.

It is the price of loving, to open one's heart
    to suffering.

As it is I can thank You for the memories they conjure up,
the rewarding companionship over the years,
    the living and doing,
    laughing and sorrowing, *together*.
The outer bond has snapped but the inner union remains,
    fanned into even brighter glow.
Praise God for memories, even if they sear
    with sudden pain.

# Moderation

Let me live with restraint, Lord,
reminding myself often that "enough is enough."
    This is good for me
for a measure of self-discipline will strengthen me.
It is so easy when one lives alone
    to indulge in small luxuries;
to over-eat, or over-sleep, or over-rest.
After all, there is no-one to criticise,
    no-one to praise or blame,
    indeed no-one to see,
    so why not?

There is a reason, Master.
The spirit must remain in charge, in authority,
or the body will take over,
    whimpering its needs and wants,
    querulously demanding cossetting,
    craving to be pampered,
drowning out the voice of reason and restraint.

Quicken my conscience, Lord, without making it
    a hard taskmaster!
After all, I have to live with it,
so I can't afford to alienate it,
Let me use moderation not as a strait-jacket,
    hampering and frustrating my movements,
but as a support, a standard, an ideal
which will lift my life above the merely material
and give me the stimulus of feeling that I am
    master over myself.
Let me repeat to myself daily that "enough is enough."

# The cupboard is bare

Master, I know I shall need a lot
for the days ahead:
courage, patience, health and much more.
As I look over my spiritual shelves
in an appraising stock-taking,
I find the cupboard is almost bare.

How can I face the lonely days, the fearful vista
of time ahead,
dwindling to a misty nothingness where even
my fertile imagination
fails to bring any clear and comforting contours?
My stock of inward resources for the future is nil,
my cupboard is bare
and my heart feels frozen and frightened.

Then You speak to me, Lord, You say:
"It has never been My plan to provide grace
in advance of need.
As you meet each new circumstance,
I shall be there,
giving you what you require.
Your cupboard will *always be empty*, but My resources
are infinite

and in the moment of need I shall respond.
Call upon Me and I shall not fail you."

So I live with my empty cupboard.
Its shelves will always be bare of spiritual stores,
but to my breast I clutch the promise of my God,
to fulfil all my needs in Christ, as they arise.

# So many of us

There are so many of us, Lord,
so many millions who pound at the gates of heaven
    tugging at Your heart-strings
    pleading with tears and promises,
    jogging Your never-failing memory
with our small individual cares.
How can You listen to us all?
How can You separate my cry from my neighbour's?
    My need from his?
To whom do You give preference if one asks sunshine
    and another rain?

Forgive us, Master, for thinking of You
    as a bigger-than-life man
    with human limitations.

You are Eternal Spirit with resources beyond
our boldest imaginings.
As there is air for all to breathe:
the newborn baby in the cot
the prisoner in the cell
the pilot of the skyborne plane
each worker along the conveyor belt,
so there is help and grace and love
flowing from You to each of us.

Your love, Master, streams towards me,
not in an impersonal cataract of mighty force,
overwhelming me with its power,
but channelled by Your tender hands to the tiny
rivulet of love
which is all that I can hold.
Let my heart, Lord, let my whole being,
be open to receive it.

## Courage for today

Lord, give me courage for today!
I dare not look ahead into the vista
of far-stretching time
or tomorrow's tasks,

but for one day, this single day,
    grant me courage, Lord.
Courage to tackle the duties to be done,
courage to face the people I must meet,
courage to hold my head high though I quail.
    Grant me quiet courage, Lord.

Let me show a brave face despite inward desolation,
    the sudden panic of aloneness,
    fears for the future,
or simply a nameless dread that grips me
    with cold clammy hands.
Grant me courage for today, Master.

Just for this day, Lord, grant me sustaining grace,
    strength for each hour that comes,
    valour when my heart feels faint;
may I sound plucky when my nerve fails.
Let me reach the evening hours having won through,
    perhaps not gloriously,
    yet adequately.
Let the thin thread of my endurance stretch
    to its utmost limits,
because it is strengthened and sustained by You.

For this one day, Lord, I pray.
    Help me through it,
and when night comes I shall thank You
    from a grateful heart.

# LOOKING FORWARD

# Growing old with grace

Help me to grow old with grace, Lord!
Even as I pray the words I smile to myself,
for grace, physical grace, is somewhat lacking
from my stiff joints and slow movements.
Gone is the limber lightness of youth,
the rapid action and supple swiftness,
each muscle part of a well-trained whole.
The years have taken their toll,
and that kind of grace is beyond me now.

It is inward grace I crave, Master,
the grace of gratitude for the past.
I call up the good moments, the joyous memories;
I relive happy scenes and savour brief triumphs.
It's been a long life but a good life.
For all this and much more, I thank You.

Then I ask, Lord, for the grace of humour.

Help me still to see the funny side of living,
to enjoy a joke
and even make one myself!
To laugh when I fumble in my purse for coins
or when memory slips a cog.

Finally, I ask for the grace of patience:
to await with hope, to endure to the end.
Not to lose out on the last lap of the race
because of flagging spirits.
Jerk me into a lively interest in my surroundings,
in the world events of the day.
Don't let me settle into a snug cocoon of self-interest.
Keep me alive and alert in mind,
even when the body no longer responds with alacrity.
Lord, help me to grow old with grace.

# Giving to You

Here I sit in my arm-chair, Master,
and I look back over my life.
What have I given You over the years?
I'm not thinking of money
for with present inflation

any sums I have given You look paltry and insignificant
today.

My mind centres on other matters.
When I was young, my days stretching out before me,
I gave You my hopes, my ambitions, my life.
In maturity I could consecrate my wider experience
to Your service.
Now that I am old, what have I to give You?
No longer can I run Your errands in service
to the lonely, needy or soul-hungry.
My voice has lost its timbre when I would tell of You;
I have so little left to offer.

I have leisure, of course, Master,
seemingly endless hours of it.
I have time to meditate, to consider Your goodness,
to trace Your plan for my life in retrospect,
wondering at Your gracious mercy and guidance.
I have time to pray,
to praise and worship,
to intercede for others.
I have never found it easy to pray in the abstract —
for Africa, China, Russia . . .
but I can name before You people under stress
who need You today,
I can bear up in prayer those whom the mass-media
bring into my horizon.

Will this be giving to You, Master?
My leisure time, my prayer, my worship?
I believe it will and that You will accept it,
for it comes from a grateful heart.

## Envy

I know the Ten Commandments, Lord,
and I have tried to follow them.
"Thou shalt not covet" . . .
but I do covet, Master, not others' houses or lands,
cars or speedboats,
but their pluck, their daring, their sheer verve
and audacity in living.
If I understand the Commandment rightly
it is possessions we must not covet;
outward things, not inward powers.
So perhaps I may be allowed to envy others
their handling of life's hard blows,
their conquering over handicaps,
their triumphant courage in face of seeming defeat.

There was that woman of eighty-one who looped the loop
up in the skies

to show she had not lost her flying skill . . .
How I admire her! I envy her courage.
Then the man of seventy-nine who gained an honours
        degree,
not afraid to study with one foot in the grave,
        to use a common expression;
though with present-day longevity one can live long
with the hypothetical foot in the non-existing grave.

O God, grant me the grit to use my days fully,
        forgetting my birthday-date
and overlooking occasional twinges of pain.
        Don't let me sit back at ease
waiting for the old spectre death to tap me on the shoulder.
Let me not only envy these brave people,
but do something in my own less drastic way to justify
        the fact of still being alive
        in a thrilling, fascinating world.
Don't take this envy from my heart, Master!
I need it as a spur to get me out of my arm-chair.

# Thoughts in the night

Sometimes I dread the night, Lord.
It stretches before me as a fearful desert
	that I must tread alone,
where shadows from the past loom as gaunt spectres
and memory empties its inmost chambers
	of half-buried grudges and failures.
What I thought forgotten becomes alive,
	takes form and voice,
scraps of conversation float in the mind,
scenes re-enact themselves with characters long dead,
and I sense again the anger, the pain, the snub,
	the crushing disappointment.

Why do these phantoms choose the night hours, Lord?
Why do they attack when my physical defences are low,
	when my mind is tired?
In the day I can ignore them
	or work them out of my system,
but in the night they assume strange power
	and threatening proportions.

Grant me peace of mind, Master, in the night hours,
	as the clock creeps slowly round.

Help me so to open my heart to Your presence
that these spectres shall skulk swiftly away,
    to the limbo where they belong.
They are fact, not fancy, but they are outgrown facts,
    situations accepted and survived,
    failures confessed and forgiven
    by others and by You.
Help me to thrust them into the past and let Your peace,
    Your wonderful pervading peace,
    fill my mind throughout the night.

## Wings

Grant me wings, Master, wings of the spirit
that will lift me right up from this chair
    and away from this room;
wings of thought that will carry me far,
out of reach of the dismal rain
    pelting down the window,
away from my crotchety old body
    proclaiming aches and pains.

Wings, Master! I crave wings,
    strong invisible wings
    on which I can fly

to where fancy beckons and thoughts beguile.
Not for me the sun-kissed beaches
hemmed in by sentinel palms,
the white surf rolling in . . .
nor for me the crowded pavements of great cities,
thronged with tourists,
gazing enraptured into the colourful shops.

Wings I would have, Lord, to land me by a country brook
babbling its peaceful way over rounded stones,
the sun glinting on the waters in a diamond display
while dragonflies skim near the surface on flashing wings.
There I would sit until peace stole into my heart,
until You came with renewing grace,
smoothing out my soul's wrinkles.
Then home again my wings would take me,
uplifted, refreshed, renewed;
ready to settle again into the comfortable chair
with a look of deep content on my face.
Wings, Lord, grant me wings!

# Packing and unpacking

I dislike packing, Master,
though I regard myself as something of an expert
after a lifetime of travelling.
The biggest difficulty is deciding what to take,
without knowing all the possible factors:
the likely weather — very important!
the possible duties — best to be prepared;
alternative routes — in case of strikes,
extra money — sure to be needed.

But even worse than packing for a journey
is the unpacking after homecoming.
Everything crumpled, creased and semi-soiled.
Why can't we have throw-away luggage
like we have disposable picnic sets?
Just imagine buying a weekend set of holiday clothes
complete in your own size,
then casting it into the dustbin before travelling home,
empty-handed but light-hearted.

My thoughts go to the final packing,
for the journey from which there is no return.
Or is it rather an unpacking, Master?

The dumping of unfulfilled hopes, of half-made plans,
of tiresome frustrations and petty vexations,
slamming the lid on a box of grudges.
Away with them all, I've finished with them . . .
then turning my face to the light,
lifting my heart to You in final yielding,
and empty-handed, passing through the veil
into the eternal spheres where You await,
My Saviour, Lord and King.

## Sunset glow

Sunset glow irradiates the sky,
and my heart is tranquil, Master, as I watch,
calmed by the pastel glories of a dying day
with the sinking sun as its radiant heart.
Then as the great orb dips below the hills
and the afterglow dies out,
I shiver a little in the night breeze.

Lord, I feel afraid,
a sense of apprehension grips me.
Must light and warmth always fade away?
Must the comfort of daylight cede to oppressive darkness?

Must sunset always follow sunrise?
        Yes, for those who watch.
But for those who follow the sun,
        there is no sunset.
For them there is continuing day.

My heart stays itself upon You, O Lord,
        upon Your tender care of me,
        Your sustaining promises.
One day for me will have no sunset.
The morning light will dawn upon this dear old world
but by evening I shall have passed beyond the sunset,
        into eternal day,
        with You, Master.

So let me enjoy each sunset glow that gladdens my eyes,
let the beauty and radiance feed my soul
with the promise of a light that never dies,
of a glory that expands, that throbs, that welcomes
        to a day that knows no end,
for there is no night in the sphere
        You are preparing for us.

# My biggest fear

Master, I can't put it into words . . .
It is a haunting phantom lurking
in the shadows of my life,
hidden from all but You.
You already know my biggest fear, that my mind
should wear out before my body.
There is a word for it but I will not whisper it,
even to You.

You did not live so long, Lord,
that this became Your problem.
The threatening symbol in Your life was a cross,
a felon's cruel death
and You met it in young manhood.
We of today live much extended lives,
cushioned from cradle to coffin by a helpful State,
and the way can be very winding and long,
tedious towards the end.

We who face the problems of the latter years,
when frailty replaces energy,
memory starts to fail
and hearing and sight diminish,
what word have You for us?

It comes so crystal clear, so convincingly true,
"Lo, I am with you all the days,
even unto the end."
We know that the physical envelope in which we live
will become old, wrinkled and worn
as it travels through the avenues of time,
but the letter inside is safe, vocal and clear
and it will reach its destination
with no single line deleted.

## Ashes

I sit at the fire of life, Master.
It has burnt down to ashes,
but it throws out a kindly warmth, agreeable
to my old bones.
Once it was newly kindled and the flames leaped high,
fanned by winds of ambition and striving,
roaring and crackling with merry force
as it devoured the kindling I heaped upon it.
Then it was good to watch, Lord!

At times an evil draught attacked it,
or the fuel I had at my command was damp...

## TOWARDS YOU, LORD

Life was not easy. There were disappointments to bear,
 sickness and conflicts to cope with.
All these had to be heaped on my fire of life.
The flickering flames turned to dark sullen smoke,
 ominous, threatening, smouldering,
 and my heart sank as I watched it.

That was long ago, Lord!
Now my fire of life has burnt down to ashes
and I have little fuel left to heap upon it.
 It must burn itself out.
It is good, though, to watch the hot grey ashes
 lit by tiny glowing gleams
showing that there is still life there.
The ashes give a comforting warmth
as I sit at ease, regarding them in reverie . . .
All gone; the long years, the storms, stresses and joys,
all consumed in the fire of life, and now only ashes left.
When the last gleam fades, You will call me
 to be with You.